How It Feels to be Adopted

Jill Krementz

How It Feels to be Adopted

Alfred A. Knopf   New York
19 🐎 83

THIS IS A BORZOI BOOK
PUBLISHED BY ALFRED A. KNOPF, INC.

Copyright © 1982 by Jill Krementz

All rights reserved under International and Pan-American Copyright Conventions. Published in the United States by Alfred A. Knopf, Inc., New York, and simultaneously in Canada by Random House of Canada Limited, Toronto. Distributed by Random House, Inc., New York

Library of Congress Cataloging in Publication Data
Krementz, Jill
How it feels to be adopted.
Summary: Interviews with adopted children and adoptive families about their experiences and feelings concerning adoption.
1. Children, Adopted—United States—Interviews.
2. Foster parents—United States—Interviews.
[1. Adoption] I. Title.
HV875.K66 1982 362.7'34'0973 82–48011
ISBN 0–394–52851–4

Manufactured in the United States of America
Published November 11, 1982
Reprinted Once
Third Printing, August 1983

For Kurt,
my very dear husband,
with love

Contents

Being adopted is different from not being adopted. As the adopted child grows up, there are special issues which arise, at home and at school, and these issues must be dealt with at various stages. Questions are asked such as: "Do I have any brothers and sisters I don't know about?" . . . "Do my birth-parents think about me on my birthday?" . . . "Are my parents happy they adopted me?" . . . "Where did my original parents come from?" and "Why couldn't they keep me?"

It becomes quickly apparent, on reading what these nineteen children have to say, that there is a broad range of feelings and attitudes among adoptees—depending on the temperament and personal situation of each child and family. Obviously, every boy and girl has his or her own way of reacting to the realities of adoption, and no one reading this book should conclude that there's a right way to react and a wrong way. My hope is that the variety of responses to the many aspects of adoption will encourage readers to realize that their own reactions are valid too and that confusion, resentment, embarrassment, curiosity, love, and gratitude are all normal and acceptable.

Adoption is certainly more openly acknowledged and discussed today than in the past. Most children now know they're adopted, whereas fifty years ago many were not told. However, many adoptees still have little information about their birthparents, and exactly how much adoptees should know about their backgrounds is a major issue. Fortunately, in my view, some agencies are now sharing more information with both adoptees and their birthparents. It is understandable that with this new openness, some new problems have surfaced—in particular, what to do about searching for birthparents. Three of the children in this book talk about just such an experience. The majority of the children I spoke to, regardless of whether or not they wanted to meet their birthparents, certainly had given the question careful thought. It was something they had pondered long before I came into their lives.

There is a lot of controversy now about whether birth records should be opened to adoptees who want to search. Mostly we have listened to the pros and cons of this subject debated by adoptive parents, directors of agencies, birthparents, psychiatrists, social workers, legislators, adult adoptees, and the media. I hope this book will provide a forum for the young adoptees as well, for their voices have not been heard. But what seems even more important than the "to search or not to search" question is the right of every adoptee who so wishes to know his or her background. Adoption agencies and those arranging private adoptions must be prepared to give out more detailed information about birthparents than they have in the past, and they should also be willing, whenever possible, to update these records. Certainly this can be done while still protecting the privacy of the birthparents.

I hope that adopted children reading this book will find themselves free to explore their own feelings openly, because whatever their questions are, I do believe it helps to talk about them. Most of the young people in this book were expressing their emotions about adoption for the first time, and they all appeared to benefit from, and enjoy, the experience. It's likely that most adoptive children have thought about the issues of adoption far more than their parents realize, and the chance to discuss all of their thoughts seemed to provide a sense of relief and pleasure. Of course, the interviewees, by virtue of the fact that their participation in this project had been left up to them by their adoptive parents, felt free to say what was really on their minds. Finding the families for this book was not easy—adoption is still a subject that makes many feel uncomfortable. It was because of the understanding and love of their parents that these children had the courage and security to explore and share their most private feelings. All of the kids, and their families, were shown their finished chapters in case they wanted to change their minds completely and not be in the book. I'm happy to say they all stayed, and for that I'm deeply grateful.

Jill Krementz

How It Feels to be Adopted

Jake, age thirteen

My parents told me that when they went to the agency to pick me up, my birthmother had dressed me in a very grown-up–looking suit with a little bow tie, even though I was only two and a half months old. It was freezing cold outside, so my father sort of stuffed me inside this big coat he was wearing so I'd stay all cozy and warm until we got home.

When I was little I couldn't really understand what being adopted meant. It was kind of hard for me to comprehend that I had another mother somewhere. It finally stuck when I was six or seven. If I adopted a child, I'd tell him he was adopted from the beginning, but I'd wait a few years to really explain the details.

I know some information about my birthmother, but not that much. I've heard what she looks like, her approximate age, and where she lived. She was very musical, quite beautiful, and just starting college when I was born. I guess she knew she was doing the right thing—that she couldn't have given me a very good life. I admire her for being able to do it because I think it takes a spe-

3

cial vision to be able to see way ahead. I mean, if you had a tiny baby, it would be easy to say, "Well, I can handle this. After all, how much room can he take?" At the time, I wasn't much bigger than a football, and could have fit into the drawer of a night table.

I don't know anything about my birthfather, and I don't wonder about him at all.

I think about being adopted, but, you know, I never really think about having another mother. I just consider the mother I have as my Mom. When I was little I used to think about my first mother more often. Whenever I got mad I'd say, "Oh, you're not my real mother—you can't punish me like that!" And my mother would say, "Yes, I *am* your real mother. Even though you had a birthmother, I am your real mother now." So as I grew older I stopped thinking things like that.

Another thing that happened when I was younger is that around Christmastime, if I had been really bad, I used to worry, Oh dear, Santa Claus isn't going to bring me any presents, he's going to put coals in my stocking, and worst of all, Mom's going to take me back to the adoption agency. Of course my parents told me it wasn't true, but I still thought it.

My little brother goes around telling everybody he's adopted. I'll be walking home from school with him and someone will say, "Oh, you two don't look anything alike," and he'll always scream out, at the top of his lungs, that we're adopted. Everyone always turns around, and it makes me blush. It also makes me want to beat him up.

Some of my friends ask me questions like I was some freak or oddball, but I just say, "What's wrong with being adopted?"

and they say, "Well, it's just that you're different," and I tell them, "No, it's not different, it's special," and after that they don't usually bring the subject up again.

Being adopted can be very embarrassing at times. For example, there's another kid I know who's adopted, and he's always getting into trouble. It really makes me upset when people say to me, "Oh, you're adopted just like him—you two should stick together!" He's a kid who talks back to teachers and writes on the wall—stuff like that. I don't even want to be near him.

I don't think I'll ever search out my birthmother. I might want to get some more facts, but I don't feel I really want to go looking. Maybe she would be awful and I'd just be disappointed. If my birthmother searched for me, I wouldn't particularly like it, but I don't think I'd mind. I'd be willing to go out for dinner with her, and I'd probably like to ask her a few questions. But I wouldn't want to stay with her or anything like that.

Carla, age twelve

Before I was adopted, I was in foster care with a black family until I was almost three years old. I had three older brothers there, and I've been told they were really nice to me, but in a way they were a little jealous because I was always favored. The foster family took me because there had been a fourth child, a little girl who died in her carriage. Everyone was so upset, and I guess they thought I could replace her in a way. But then my foster mother was in an accident, and when she went to the hospital, my foster father couldn't handle me by himself. I was looked at by a lot of black families who wanted to adopt, but no one wanted me because I seemed so attached to the family I was with and they didn't want to take me away from them. When I was finally adopted by the white family I have now, it was probably because they saw me in a different setting, without my foster family.

Sometimes my friends say I act white, but I don't think you can act white or black. Sometimes I feel funny when I'm the only black person in a group of white people, but most times I don't notice it. It doesn't matter to me what color my friends are, as long as they're nice to me and nice to other people.

I don't think about being adopted all that much. Once in a while I do, and that's usually when I'm mad at my mother. Sometimes when I'm really mad, I'll daydream about what it would be like to be living with my real mother—with the lady I was born from. I don't usually say anything; I just keep it in my head. But I don't really think of my birthmother as my real mother, because it's the mother I have now who takes care of me when I'm sick and who's always there when I need her. She acts just like a real mother to me. She doesn't treat me any differently than she does her other children. My parents have four kids in all—two are adopted and two are not.

It would probably be dangerous not to tell your child she's adopted, but I think it's OK if I just pretend I'm not. But parents should always tell the truth. They should never lie to you.

There is one time when I do always think about my biological mother, and that's on my birthday. I've never skipped a year without wondering, How does she feel on this day? Does she think of me, or does she just pretend that I was never born and it's any other day? Is she sad, or is she happy? I hope that she does think about me, and I hope she wonders what I'm like, how I am, what I look like, how I act, and things like that. I would imagine that she *would* remember and think about me and that it might be a hard time for her. If we should ever meet each other, there's one question I'd like to ask her: How does she feel on my birthday?

I don't really wonder about my birthfather. Sounds weird, but I never do.

Being adopted is not something I talk about all that much. Sometimes my sister and I will talk. She says she doesn't want to look for her birthmother when she gets older, but I still have mixed feelings. Sometimes I feel that I want to look for her—and my mother says she'll help me when I'm older—but sometimes I don't want to look for her at all because I'm scared of finding out what her reactions would be. I worry that she'll have a whole new life and I'll just be interfering with that new life. She might not want anyone to know about her past. But other times I want to look for her.

If my birthmother wanted to meet me sometime, that would be OK, but I would want to stay where I am right now. I'm happy here. I worry that it would make me feel caught in the middle, and I wouldn't want that to happen.

When I grow up, I think I'd like to adopt one or two children. It would make me feel good to know I could make another person happy the way my family's made me happy. Another reason I'd like to is because if I hadn't been adopted I'd still be in a foster home.

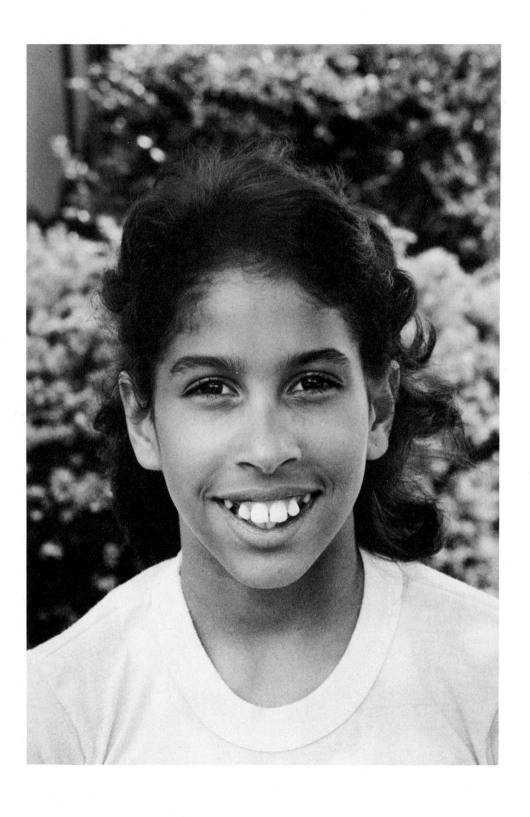

Melinda, age ten

After I was born I stayed with my mother until I was three. Then she put me in the orphanage because she couldn't take care of me—she didn't even have enough money to pay her rent. She wasn't married so it was really hard for her. At first I cried all the time because I was so lonesome and I hated being separated from my Mommy, but after a few months I got used to it and had fun playing with the other kids.

By the time I was four, I had moved into a foster home where I stayed until I was seven. That's where I met my real sister, Lauren, who was only a few months old and had been placed with the same foster family. She's probably my half-sister because I doubt we have the same father. There was another little girl living there too, named Irma, who was four years older than me.

When I was six, I found out that I had a little brother, Julio, who had been sent to live with another foster family. I only met him once. It's hard to believe my mother kept having so many children when she couldn't take care of them, but I guess she kept thinking things would get better.

I loved my foster parents and I was always hoping they would adopt me and Lauren. They never did. They finally moved to Puerto Rico and took Irma with them, but not us. I wasn't too upset because we both got adopted before they left.

The parents I have now found us by going to an agency and asking if there was a little girl who needed a warm and loving home. The agency people said they had *two* little girls named Lauren and Melinda who would be perfect for them. So we all met each other at the agency and played for a few hours. They had already adopted a little baby boy named Adam and they brought him along. The next week Lauren and I went for a sleepover at their house and I have a photograph from that night which I keep in my wallet. It's one of my most precious possessions because that's the night they decided to keep us. It was just after supper when we were all sitting around the table and they told us that from now on we could call them Mom and Dad. They said it wouldn't be like a fairy tale because everyone would have to work real hard to make the family work—that we would all have to pitch in and try to help each other. But all I was thinking was how much I loved them already and I couldn't wait to be part of a real family. I didn't care how much work I had to do.

Two months later we had a big party and Lauren and I met about a zillion new relatives. That was great, and I can't even remember all the cousins I met that day.

The past three years have been terrific, but I can't say there haven't been some problems. For example, Lauren and I didn't speak English very well so I had a hard time keeping up with my classmates. It was easier for Lauren because she was just

learning to talk anyway. And I had a lot of new things to learn—
little things like how to pay for my lunch at school, because I
had never done that before. For the first week I only bought pea-
nuts and ice cream. My new parents got suspicious when I kept
telling them how great the school lunches were. They didn't believe me. Then they figured out what was going on!

I guess the hardest thing for me in the first year was when I had to go back to the agency for follow-up visits. I was always terrified that I would see my other mother there and she would want to take me home with her again. That's because when I was in foster care we had monthly visits—my mother and I—in the playroom at the agency.

My Mom, the one who adopted me, is Puerto Rican and so are both her parents. I'm especially happy about that, because Lauren and I are both Puerto Rican and it's fun to keep in touch with our real background. My Grandma has taught us how to cook all different kinds of Spanish foods. Adam likes the tasting part. Sometimes we go there for sleepovers and that's a lot of fun. At first I wouldn't stay overnight because I was afraid that my parents would never come back to get us.

Dad's Greek and his favorite expression is "S'agapo poli," which means "I love you very much." When we were studying Greek mythology in my class I brought in lots of his books. We go to St. George's Greek Orthodox Church every Sunday, and what's best of all is that we have two Easters—one Catholic and one Greek.

My new Mom used to work full time, but she doesn't anymore so she can give Lauren and me and Adam a lot of extra attention. I appreciate that, because the first seven years weren't too easy for me. I've never had real parents until now and it's hard for me not to feel a little insecure if one of them isn't around. I wish they could both be here all the time, but of course somebody has to work. It would be nice if we could get money from the sky, but I haven't seen any dollar bills floating down like rain. Mom says if I find any to let her know.

Sometimes I think about my first mother—like I wonder if she's lonely and if she's worked out all her problems. I hope she has a better life. It must be hard for her not to have her kids and it would be nice if the agency people told her what a happy life Lauren and I have now. Now that the adoption is final, I'd like to see her again. I still remember what she looks like—she has short brown hair and brown eyes and she looks just like me. I don't think much about Julio because Adam's my brother now.

Whenever I watch television and see those programs about foster children who need homes I think about how lucky I am, and I wish they could all be adopted. All kids need a home they can call their very own.

Timmy, age twelve

I was adopted when I was about three days old. My birthmother was sixteen, and I don't know how old the guy was. My parents brought me home directly from the hospital. The only information I have about my background is that my birthmother was Catholic and wanted me placed with a Catholic family.

I was told I was adopted when I was about two, but I had no idea what it meant. When my parents said, "You're adopted," I thought they were saying, "You're a doctor," and I kept telling them, "No, I am *not* a doctor!" I hated the idea of being a doctor because I hated doctors. I still hate them because I can't stand shots.

When I was three, my sister, Rebecca, was born, and that's when I realized where babies come from. My Mom explained that being adopted meant I grew in somebody else's tummy, so it was at this time that I started asking any woman who came into the house if I had grown inside *her* tummy. I must have made a complete fool of myself.

The first time I really thought about being adopted was in fourth grade, when we studied a story in our reading book about a girl who was adopted. I told my teacher I was adopted, too, but she didn't believe me because I look so much like my parents. She asked my mother, and Mom told her, yes, I was adopted. That was the first time that the kids in my school knew.

Some of my friends asked me dumb questions, like "Did your parents die?" or "Why didn't they want you?" I think they probably *did* want me, but they were so young they would have had to drop out of school, and it would have cost a lot of money to raise me—to buy food, diapers, clothes, and stuff like that. The older I get, the easier it is for me to understand—I mean, right now I'm just four years younger than she was, and it would be impossible for me to try and bring up a kid. I know I'd be so tired from waking up in the middle of the night that I'd never get to school! And if I paid someone else to baby-sit, I'd have to sell my foreign-coin collection. I get $1.50 a week allowance, and in the summer I weed around the house for some extra money, but I don't think that would go very far. And I'd have to get rid of my cat because, believe me, she'd get into the baby's milk, for one thing, and secondly, she's used to getting a lot of attention, so she'd be very jealous.

Sometimes I feel jealous of my younger sister because she's not adopted and she doesn't have to answer questions about it. That's the only difference, though. We get treated the same, except I probably get in more trouble because I'm older and I tease her a lot.

When I was younger, if I got really mad at my parents, I'd say stuff like "You're not my real Mom and Dad, and I should be with another family," but I don't do that anymore. When they yell at me, I realize that they *are* my parents and they can scold me all they want.

Actually, I don't think about being adopted all that often—maybe two or three times a year. Like, I wonder how it would have felt if I had been adopted by a poor family and I only had one piece of stale bread a day to eat. Or I wonder what it would be like to be with a really rich family and have a Ferrari and a swimming pool.

I don't particularly want to meet my birthparents. The only part I'm curious about is what they look like, and I'd like to know what kind of grades they got. I don't think meeting each other is a good idea, because you just don't know what could happen and it could turn into a tragic situation. Someone could get their feelings hurt, and it would probably be me because I'd be caught in the middle.

Sue, age thirteen

I was told that I was adopted as soon as I was old enough to understand what it meant. My sister and two brothers, all older, are also adopted, and they have all searched for and found their birthparents. I was always a little jealous of them, and I wondered if one day I would have a chance to search, too. I was promised from the beginning that my parents would help me when I got old enough, which would probably be when I was eighteen. But then, when I was twelve, we moved from Pennsylvania to New Jersey, and it was at that time that my mother wrote to the bureau of statistics for my original birth certificate. Pennsylvania is one of the few states that have open records, which means that adoptees eighteen and over, or their adoptive parents, can get information about birthparents.

Most adoptive parents today aren't open enough with their adoptive kids. As a result, the adoptees don't totally understand what adoption is, and therefore they're mixed up about whether they should search or not. It never really occurred to me, at any age, that I wasn't mature enough to look for my birthmother, and I wanted to as soon as we got my records. My older sister, Cindy, and her friend Debbie did most of the detective work and located her address and phone number on December 1, five days before my thirteenth birthday.

The next morning, while I was at school, my Mom telephoned my birthmother and said, "I am calling with loving understanding for the common bond we share—our daughter, born December 6, 1968." They both cried a lot, and when I got home from school that afternoon, my Mom put her arms around me and told me about their talk. Then, on my thirteenth birthday, my birthmother called me and we talked for about fifteen minutes. It was kind of hard getting on the phone with a total stranger and carrying on a normal conversation, but it was just the fact that she was on the other end that mattered. It was a neat feeling. The only part that was hard on me was afterwards—waiting for her to send me some pictures of herself. I was dying to find out what she looked like, and I think she took a long time because she was worried that she looked terrible and that I wouldn't be proud of her. She just wanted everything to be perfect. Waiting to hear from her, and having to wait so long, was the one thing I didn't like about finally finding her. It really bothered me.

When she did write, she told me that she'd lost contact with my birthfather the last couple of years, but she would try and find him for me. If I do eventually contact him, he may not be as open as she was because he was supposed to marry her and didn't, so he might feel guilty. Also, my birthmother had told everyone in her family that she had surrendered a child for adoption when she was twenty-two, so when I contacted her it was a shock, but it wasn't all that complicated. She said that she had gotten mar-

ried to someone else after I was born, but that she was divorced now and living with her two sons, one fourteen and one sixteen. She had them when she was married for the first time, at seventeen, before she got divorced and had me. So that means I have four brothers! I've got pictures of my half-brothers, and all my girl friends are begging for an introduction.

My birthmother called me again on Christmas Day, and we've corresponded two, maybe three times. We're hoping to meet her in Pittsburgh this summer.

I have a friend who lives next door, and when I showed him the pictures of my birthmother, he asked me, "Are you going to move back down to Florida now?" And I laughed really hard and said, "That just goes to show that some people don't understand—when you're adopted by people, these people are your real parents. Finding your birthmother is just filling up a gap that makes you feel you belong."

The fact that my parents were so supportive of my searching was wonderful to me. My Mom has always been active in the adoption movement to open records so it's natural for me to think that way. But even if they hadn't helped, I'm sure I would eventually have gone on a search of my own. I don't know how I would have done it, but I would have tried, and I'm confident I would have found other people willing to help me.

The thing that bothers me is that nobody ever listens to kids—to *their* feelings. It's always the birthparents, the adoptive parents, and the adoptees over eighteen who do all the talking. People think that kids under eighteen aren't mature enough to understand their own feelings.

I think adopted kids should be allowed to search whenever they're ready. They need to know where they came from, instead of thinking that they just appeared on this earth from outer space and were adopted by somebody. And they need to know what their medical history is. But the main reason is because everyone goes through an identity crisis at one time or another and everyone needs to know where he or she came from. As soon as I searched and found the information I was looking for, I felt more worthwhile in the world—as though I belonged better. Beforehand, a part of me had always been missing.

Even if I had found something disturbing at the end of the search—like her life was a total disaster or she was dead—just knowing that I had found the person I was looking for would have been important to me. But don't get me wrong—I'm glad that I found her, and I'm happy she's alive and well.

I think some people are against searching because they think their birthmothers don't want anyone to know they surrendered a baby. But that kind of thinking goes back to the olden days whe it was considered a sin for a young teenager to get pregnant and so everyone kept it a secret. It's just not that way anymore. Another reason people want closed records is because the adoptive parents feel really threatened. They think that when adoptees find their birthparents they'll love them less or want to leave. But that's simply not going to happen. To tell you the truth, I think the relationship between adoptive parents and adoptees would improve with open records because the adoptee would have a better attitude knowing that he or she truly belonged and that there wasn't a missing part anymore.

Being adopted has always been a very positive experience for me. Of course there have been times when it hasn't been all that great, like when I've gotten really mad at my parents and have felt like just turning around and saying, "I wish I wasn't adopted by you! If you yell at me as much as you do, and if you don't love me, then why did you adopt me? Why don't you just give me up for adoption again?" I've never said it, because I know it would hurt them, and me, too, but I've sure thought it from time to time.

But, all in all, I'm proud of being adopted. It seems strange to say it, but it makes me stick out from other people—makes me different. I'm not ordinary. I've developed much better relationships with my teachers because when they found out I was adopted they asked me all kinds of questions and they've been very interested in my search. And since I found my birthmother, all my grades have gone way up!

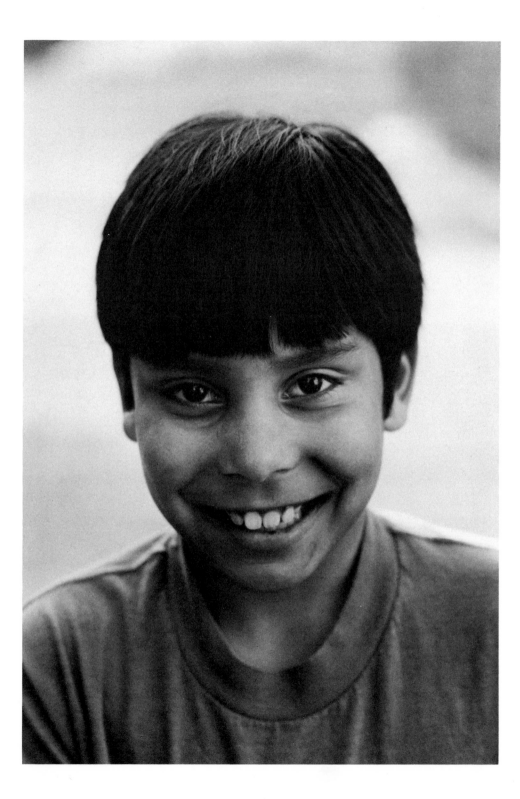

Matt, age nine

My parents wanted to adopt a baby boy, and one day they got a phone call from someone who asked if they would like a little Indian boy. They said they would *love* one, and so that's how they got me. They had to sign a lot of papers, and then they became my parents.

I was five months old at the time. My real mother wasn't able to provide for me, and she thought that the most loving thing she could do for me was to place me with a family who could take care of me.

I know a little about my Indian background, which is that I'm descended from three of the civilized tribes in the Southeast— the Seminole, the Choctaw, and the Chickasaw. Whenever I look in the atlas at the state where I was born, I always wonder which of the little towns I'm from.

I don't have the foggiest idea where I was actually born or who my parents were. Sometimes I think about it at night, because I have a picture of an Indian chief hanging on my wall. I wonder

what my real parents looked like and what kind of a house they lived in when I was born. I don't think they lived in a teepee, because they blow away too easily. I imagine they lived in a small one-story house without electricity. Sometimes I imagine what it would be like to still be living on the reservation—I probably wouldn't have a TV or a radio, so that would be a real pain! The way my Mom described them, from what the agency people told her, my real father was about six-foot and my mother was five-eleven, so I'll probably be tall when I grow up.

I might like to meet my Indian parents someday, but I don't think about it all that much. I usually have other things on my mind—like doing my homework or meeting a friend. And I imagine they're probably busy, too, doing other things.

I do wish my skin color was a little bit lighter. I don't like getting a tan in May while school is still going on, because the kids tease me and call me names like "Brownie" or "Chocolate Chip," and this hurts my feelings. If they're my age, I either punch them or tell my parents, but if they're younger, I let it go. The first time it made me cry, but my sister Beth was with me and she helped me to feel better. She told me to try and ignore them. Most of the time, though, they don't tease me; in fact, they make me feel special and proud to be the only full Indian in my school. Whenever anyone in my class asks questions about Indian history, I'm usually the person who knows the answers. Even though I don't know that much about my individual history, I know a lot more than my friends do about my overall past. I know it sounds funny to say, but even though I'm adopted, and on top of that a completely different race from my parents and sisters, it just never occurs to me that they're not my real family!

Barbara, age sixteen

Mother's Day is a kind of wonderful day in our house—between my mother and myself. We've got a different relationship than most people because I'm adopted. If I do something special for her on that day, it makes her more happy than most mothers since, I guess, there's always a fear on her part that I'm not going to think of her as my mother. But I do, because she's the one who has raised me and because she's such a terrific person. I never think of my natural mother on Mother's Day.

Holidays and birthdays are all good days for us as an adopted family. It's almost like we passed a test or something, like we're better than the rest, more unique, because my parents chose me, my sister, and my brother; they didn't just end up with us. We are the children they wanted, and that's neat!

Having an older brother and sister who are also adopted has always made it a lot easier for me. My brother rarely thinks about it, but it's bothered my sister some. It's sort of been an excuse for her to be a rebel—like, the world left her alone, so she's going to rebel against it.

I don't know anything, really, about my natural parents, and that upsets me a lot. All I know is that I was adopted when I was thirteen months old. I know I lived in a foster home and they called me Joy because I didn't have a legal name and I was a joy to have in the house. There's a real temptation for me to say, "Yeah, I remember the house—it was gray—and I remember the people," but I don't, really. It's hard to know the difference between what I remember and what I've been told.

Sometimes I make up stories about my early childhood, about those first thirteen months, because I just desperately want to have a part of my life that's entirely mine, my very own. Being adopted, I often feel that everything I've got, including my name, has been given to me by my adoptive parents. So if I have some memories, even if they're fantasies, I guess it's because I need to feel that I came to my parents with something that was already mine.

Being adopted can be embarrassing—like when people start talking about their nationalities and you just have to be quiet. You can't say anything, because you don't know. I've just gotten in the habit of saying, "My mother's Polish, my father's Irish," and I leave it at that. That's my adoptive parents' background I'm talking about. I don't know what I really am, and that bothers me; all my friends know what they are, and it makes me feel very jealous of them. If I worked at an adoption agency, it would bother me to know I was sending out all these little babies without any information about their past.

When I think about being adopted, not knowing why and trying to understand why—with no information—I just get really

mad. Usually the anger is directed at my natural parents. And I'd say it's directed more at my birthmother than at my birthfather.

My thoughts about my birthmother are, generally speaking, not too good. In a way, I can understand that a baby can come into your life at the wrong time and it's just impossible to see raising this child. But if you think about the child, you really are just walking away from it and leaving it with nothing—regardless of the circumstances. If I was put up for adoption for a good reason—to help the woman who carried me—then I think that from the start they should have told me that. It's when you're not told anything that you think it's got to be something lousy—like, she didn't want the kid and all she was in it for was the fun beforehand. I can't go along with that. My sister, who is divorced and very young, has two tiny children, and my parents are taking care of them while she gets herself back together. I think that's great, and I think other young mothers with kids should try to work out this kind of alternative—looking for help from parents or relatives so they can keep their child. I'm basically against giving a child away, but I'm very glad there are people like my parents who want to adopt children.

As for my birthfather, I don't feel very good about him, either. When I see my friends with their fathers—and especially when I look at my own family with my own father—what I see is how much that man is loving his family, so happy to be there and *wanting* to be there. And I wonder, What kind of man could not want to be part of all this loving and caring? What kind of man could walk out of a situation like this?

No, I don't particularly want to meet my birthparents, and I doubt that I ever will. I know I'd only want to tell them how I'm feeling, and since that obviously wouldn't help them, why disrupt their lives even more? As far as I'm concerned, the mother and father I have now are my family. They're the ones I love and who love me.

I suppose that being adopted and feeling the way I do about my natural parents has definitely given me a lower self-image than a lot of people have. And yet, all my friends see me as joking and laughing—playing around and having a good time; they don't really see that I'm not as happy as I look. What's good about my situation? I'm part of a very loving family, and I'm probably more in touch with my real feelings than a lot of kids my age are.

Alfred, age fourteen

I've been told that when I was only a few months old my biological father died in the Vietnam war. My mother couldn't take care of me, so she put me into foster care, where I stayed until I was eight. My foster parents said they wanted to adopt me, but they never did and I'm just as glad because I wasn't very happy there anyway. I felt they treated me unfairly at times. They thought I was a year older than I actually was and so they pushed me to do a lot of things I wasn't capable of doing.

The father I have now—his name is James—found me when he was working for the New York Council on Adoptable Children. One day he was looking through one of their books which had pictures of adoptable kids and he saw this cute little boy—me—who he thought he would like to adopt. I was eight at the time. He wasn't married but he had already adopted one child, Wayne, who is a year older than I am. James asked Wayne if he'd like a brother to keep him company and Wayne said, "Sure." One day a social worker came to see me at my foster home and showed me photographs of James and Wayne and said this family was interested in adopting me. About a week later the three of us met at McDonald's for dinner because that was Wayne's favorite restaurant, and we all got along fine. After that evening I visited them a couple of times for the weekend to give Wayne a chance to decide whether he really wanted me to stay or whether he wanted to change his mind, because the final outcome was going to have to be a joint decision between Wayne and James. I enjoyed the visits a lot, and I was praying they would adopt me. At the same time, I was preparing myself for rejection, you know, because if they decided not to keep me I didn't want it to hit me by surprise. My foster parents had often said they would adopt me, and just when I'd get my hopes up, they would change their minds at the last minute. So over the years I've learned to take things in stride.

About a month later, the first week of September, the social worker told me to pack my bags, that I was going to move in with my new adoptive family—that this time it would be forever. My foster parents drove me to the agency, and my new Dad was waiting there to take me home. When we drove up to the house, there was a big poster on the front door which said:

WELCOME HOME

ALFRED!

Wayne was waiting for us, and as soon as he saw the car, he ran out to help us with my bags. It had to be the happiest day of my life.

The past six years have been great for me. My Dad has adopted three more boys—Russell who is Korean, Paul who is bi-racial, and Louis who is Hispanic. At times I don't know how Dad copes with all of us, because we're typical teenagers and we can

be a pretty rowdy bunch. Besides that, we do eat a lot! He's a
great cook and he's taught all of us how to do some of the cook-
ing. One thing we've learned from him is how to shop economi-
cally. I admit there have been times when I wanted my father to
get married because we were getting into a lot of mischief and I
felt he was having trouble controlling us—we were just too much
for him to handle alone. There were days when I'd *beg* him:
"Get married, Dad, so you can have somebody here at all times
and keep us in shape—keep us out of trouble." He said, "Getting

married won't fulfill my life and getting married won't stop the problems either. I feel fine as I am." At first I felt he was just trying to prove a point saying that he could take care of five kids without a wife. But actually he has proved it, because in my opinion he's doing a great job. In fact, a lot of people envy him—that he can have such a rewarding life as a single person with children—and I'm very proud of him. I know he has some relationships, but he keeps them a secret.

I'm glad I was placed with a black father, because black people have a different culture. I think it's easier for everyone. On the other hand, I have a Korean brother and a Hispanic one, and it works out fine. At first it didn't because they were all so different: Russell dressed with all kinds of funny colors and ate with chopsticks. And Louis was always asking for Spanish food. But slowly they've adjusted to our way of life and we've adjusted to theirs. We call ourselves The Rainbow Family.

As for my real mother, I don't think about her anymore and it's not a subject I like to talk about. I don't know where she is and I figure that if she really wants to know where I am, she'll make an attempt to find me. I understand what her intentions were—that she simply couldn't take care of me—and I don't hold it against her. I'm just glad I ended up where I am now.

My Dad and I get along so well, and have so much in common, it's as if we're on the same wavelength. Maybe it's because we both have the same birthday—we were both born on December 18, and he was born exactly thirty years before me. We have a very tight relationship, my father and I. Actually, we're so much alike that I usually forget I'm adopted.

Holly, age fifteen

At about one-thirty in the afternoon, the telephone rang, and the voice on the other end asked for my mother. It was a Saturday and I was home alone. I said she was out, so the caller asked me to write down her name, address, and telephone number, which I did. Then the woman who was on the other end of the phone said, "Fourteen years ago I had a baby that I gave up for adoption. I believe you are my daughter."

I was in total shock, and as we talked, my mind was in a different world. She asked me a lot of questions about myself and filled me in on what had happened to her. She said she was five-foot-four, had blond hair and green eyes, and that she worked for a management consulting company. And she explained why she had put me up for adoption. She was seventeen when she met and fell in love with my birthfather, but by the time she found out she was pregnant they had broken up. She wanted to keep me, but her mother talked her out of it. She told me she had gotten married since then, to someone else, but was presently divorced and she didn't have any other kids. We talked for about an hour, and after I hung up I started sobbing. One of my father's friends, Mike Rodgers, came in the door looking for my parents, and I put my arms around him and just kept on crying and crying. I couldn't stop.

I wasn't crying because I was sad. I had planned on searching when I got a little older, and my parents were going to help me. In fact, it was something we had talked about very recently. So I was happy that my birthmother had found me, but I never expected it to be so all-of-a-sudden. I always figured I had till tomorrow—you know, a few years more before I really had to deal with it.

I was finally able to tell Mike about the phone call, and he drove me over to where my mother—my adoptive mother—was working. On the way over we met my Dad, but I was still crying so hard I couldn't explain what had happened—I couldn't get the words out of my mouth. He thought someone had died until I was finally able to tell him, and then he didn't know what to say. I had to leave for a basketball game at school, so he went and picked up Mom at work, told her to sit down, and told her everything. When I got home from the game, we all talked and decided it would be best to begin a relationship slowly—that we would just exchange information and photographs by mail for a while. That's what we did for about two months. I was still wandering around in a daze during this time, and I was worried about how my life might change. My mother said I should just think of Alison, my birthmother, as a friend, and that I should try to put myself in her position, so that's what I tried to do. And then in May we finally met. We invited Alison to stay with us for a few days, and she flew out for a weekend visit. My parents and I met her at the airport, and that was really weird. I was glad we were a little bit late because that gave us something to talk about while we were walking through the terminal. After we got to our house she gave me a picture of my birthfather and also the little bracelet they had put on my wrist when I was born. She had kept it all these years.

We spent the weekend mostly talking about what she had been doing since I was born and how she had found me. It took her eight months and a lot of work, calling around and checking records. I showed her my scrapbook and told her about my school—stuff like that. We didn't go out anywhere, and I didn't

get a chance to introduce her to any of my friends. We had a
good visit, and after she left, we wrote letters back and forth.

The following month, after school got out, I went to visit her
for a week. That was really exciting because I had never been to
New York before, but it upset me when her friends would say
stuff like "So you're Alison's daughter." I didn't know what to
say. I sort of went along with it because I didn't know what else
they could call me, but by not saying anything, I felt like I was
taking away something from my Mom. It's confusing because I
don't know how to categorize my relationship with Alison. I
don't want to think of it as purely biological, but I don't know

how else to define it. I feel ridiculous introducing her as "my friend," and yet I certainly don't think of her as my mother. Nor do I want to. In my view I have only one mother and that's the mother who raised me and mothered me—who gave me food and shelter and love while I was growing up. That's my definition of a mother. My birthmother's the person who gave me my heredity and my life, and while I don't want to push her away, I also don't want to take anything away from my Mom. I don't want my mother to feel any loss of prestige.

One thing that's nice about Alison—it's a part of her that I really enjoy—is that she loves to do new things like ice-skating or trying new restaurants. My Mom, who isn't particularly adventurous, says this is good for me. She wants me to have new experiences and grow as a person. I know she probably feels a little threatened by Alison, who's ten years younger than she is, but I think she's so secure about herself as a person that she can handle it. And since I tend to be somewhat shy, it has been great for me to travel a little and spread my wings. Still, I prefer having Alison visit us. She flew down again this Easter for a week, and I felt much more comfortable and secure in my own environment. Last winter, when I went to see her, I felt my parents were trying to push me away. I know they were just trying to be nice and let me know I was free to visit her for however long I wanted—that it wouldn't hurt their feelings or make them feel rejected—but instead of making me feel free, it made me worry that they didn't love me, that they were rejecting me!

The past two years have been real hard on my parents. I get the feeling that sometimes they're thinking that they're losing me, and that's the last thing in the world I want them to feel. It isn't true. And most of all, I don't want to lose them. Once, when my mother and I were having a fight—the way all mothers and daughters have arguments—my Mom said something like "Well, you can just go and live with Alison." Even though I knew she didn't mean it, I felt really hurt. That's the sort of thing that can't ever be said—not in the heat of an argument, and not even joking around.

I think I'm probably mature for my age, so I've been able to handle all of this fairly well. But that initial phone call was definitely a bad idea. If I was a birthmother and I had a fourteen-year-old daughter, I'd probably go through her parents first. And if I was scared that her parents wouldn't let me talk to her, or possibly wouldn't even tell her I'd called and would just send me a lawyer's letter telling me to get lost, then I'd try to use an intermediary. Calling directly is just too big a shock for a kid. The whole notion of searching is still pretty new, and it's hard for anyone to know how to act, so I'm not mad at Alison and I *am* glad she found me. That's all in the past. Right now we have to deal with the future, and my main concern is that Alison may expect more out of me than I can give. It would be sad if she wanted to make me the center of her existence, because I can't do the same thing for her. I want to be friendly but I don't want anything past that. I know where she is and what she looks like, and that's great, but it's all I ever wanted or needed.

Alison and I have talked about this and she told me I don't need to worry—that any relationship is determined by mutual consent. She says all she wants is for us to be honest and open with each other, and no matter what happens, just knowing that I'm alive and well is wonderful for her. I hope that's true because right now I'm feeling real protective about my Mom and I'd hate to feel I have two mothers. I'd like to keep in touch with Alison, but anything beyond that is too much of a responsibility for me. We've each got our own life to live.

Quintana, age sixteen

My parents once met a very nice doctor at a party, and one day when I was about twelve hours old, this same doctor phoned my parents. My Dad answered the phone because my Mom was in the shower, and the doctor said, "Do you want to adopt a little baby girl?" My Mom started crying because she was so happy, and they both ran to the hospital to see me. I was in this room with a lot of other babies, and I had a little bracelet on which said "NI," meaning "no information." My Dad always used to joke about this part when I was little. He said he wandered up and down the aisles of the nursery, stopping beside each tiny bassinet, saying, "No, not this one. . . . No, not that one," until finally he stopped beside me and said, "*She's* the one!" Of course that's not how it really happened, but I love the story.

My parents have referred to me as *adoptada* for as long as I can remember. But I didn't understand exactly what it meant until I was ten or eleven. And then I started thinking about it a lot. It's definitely better if kids know about being adopted from the beginning so that it doesn't come as a big shock later on.

My birthmother was eighteen when I was born, and my birthfather was twenty-one. I've always thought they gave me up for my own good, because they were just too young to take care of me and because they probably weren't married. I've never thought of it as any sort of insult to me. I don't imagine them still being together after all this time, but I do see them as still being very young, so when I get into arguments with my parents, I think maybe my *real* parents would be more understanding. It's a terrible thing for me to do, and I've never said anything about it.

I call my birthmother my *real* mother, and sometimes I call her my other mother. The parents I have now are my mother and my father.

I sometimes picture all the different kinds of families I could have been adopted into. I wonder what it would have been like if I'd gotten adopted into some family in another country with a different culture, or, you know, what if I'd been adopted by a family in Kansas or something.

I visualize my birthmother as being really tall—I don't know why, because I'm not all that tall—and I can sing pretty well, so it's possible that I inherited some musical ability. My parents always tell me that I have a great ability to sense things that are going on, like observing other people the way a writer does; and if that's true, then that's a quality that probably emerged from the way I was brought up, because my parents are both writers.

The only time being adopted has been any kind of a problem is when I'm sitting in biology class and we're talking about genes and the teacher asks us to trace back our grandparents and do things like family trees. I just do the best I can and work out the

genealogy with the parents I'm living with now. But while I'm doing the assignment, I am thinking there's really no point in doing it, because it's not true.

My parents have always been willing to talk to me, whenever I want to, about my being adopted. They've told me everything they know about my birthmother, and they've always told me that if I ever want to look for her, they'll help me in any way and contact lawyers and all that. I'm not sure yet if I want to find her, but if I ever do, I'll probably be able to, because I know her name and roughly where she's from. Having so much information has made me more curious in a way, and sometimes it even makes me feel that maybe I *should* follow through. But then I worry that maybe my real mother doesn't want me to look for her for some reason—maybe it was a terrible time in her life that she wants to forget. Maybe she feels guilty about giving me up. I wouldn't want to intrude.

In a way, I don't think I'll ever meet her if I haven't by now. And I think if she hasn't contacted me by now, she never will. I'm getting less curious every year, and one reason might be because I don't really have much time to do a lot of detective work. I was more interested when I was eleven or twelve.

I never imagine a reunion in terms of her finding me. I mean, I'd love to see her if she found me, and it would be a lot easier, but I'd be more satisfied with myself if I'd taken the time to find her. It would be a bigger accomplishment and more of an adventure.

Someone once asked me what I would do if I found my real mother, and I said, "I would put one arm around Mom and one arm around my other Mommy, and I'd say, 'Hello, Mommies.' "

Philip, age fifteen

I've always known I was adopted, and when I was real little, I would go up to every pregnant lady I saw and ask her if she was planning to keep her baby or to give it up for adoption. They would all just stop dead in their tracks and look at me as though I were crazy.

The other thing I did that made people think I was a little strange was that just before my family adopted Jack, I kept telling everyone I was going to have a new baby brother. They kept saying, "You don't know, dear. You might have a baby sister." And I kept telling them, "Yes, I *do* know," because my parents had told the agency which sex they wanted.

I never thought about being adopted until I was in the fifth grade and we were studying reproduction in science class. We started talking about eyes and how if both parents have blue eyes the kids can't have brown eyes. Well, as it turns out, both my parents have blue eyes, and Jack and I both have brown eyes, so that's when it really hit me, in a sense. I had actually forgotten about being adopted up until then. It's a good thing my parents had told me, because it would have been an awful way to find out—I would have felt terrible. Now that I know a little more about genetics, I figure that there are probably quite a few kids in my school who are adopted but who don't admit it—sort of old-timey types whose families think adoption is something to be done discreetly, in secret.

I don't think about my birthparents very much. I certainly have never imagined them as being together—not now or even when I was born. I mean, why would they give up their child for adoption if they were together and married? I certainly don't think they gave me up for purely economic reasons, because I don't think money is all that important when you're making that kind of a decision. I figure my mother was just a teenager who got pregnant. Simple as that!

I keep seeing these dumb movies on TV about searching, and my feeling is that going into the past is not very wise. You could wind up in a lot of trouble. I also think it could be hard on your adoptive parents because they might feel that they weren't loved. If it's really, really important for you to search, then I'd say you should wait until you're older and not totally living at home with your parents—when you're twenty-one, twenty-two. If I ever did decide to search, I would hope that I had some sort of stability as a person before I started digging into my past. As for birthparents' searching, I don't know how I feel about that. I assume they gave up their kids for a good reason, and if they didn't—well, I hate to blame them, but it truly is their fault, and they don't have the right to reexamine their decision later on. I think it could create a lot of problems. I know I would definitely feel caught in the middle.

So far, the only real problem I have with being adopted relates to my being part of a Jewish family. Whenever I go to temple or when we celebrate the Sabbath on Friday night, I often sense that there's a Hebrew loyalty that my relatives have that I don't. Even though people tell me that my natural parents were Jewish, in my heart I'm just not all that certain. I mean, how do I know that they were both really Jewish? How do I know that my real mother didn't fall in love with a Roman Catholic or something?

The best thing about being adopted is that I can have wonderful fantasies about my birthmother. And if you're a dreamer, which I can be, your mother can become anyone you want her to be. I happen to like opera a lot, so for a while my real mother was Maria Callas. She was such a strange and wonderful lady, and I thought it was neat to have such a bizarre and exotic mother. She's dead now. She never found out what a crazy son she had!

Jack, age twelve

Being adopted hasn't really affected my life all that much. Some of the kids at school used to make a big production out of it, but I didn't pay any attention to them. Sometimes they'd ask me a lot of questions like "Are you adopted?" and I'd say "Yes." Then they'd ask me if I'd like to know who my real parents are and I'd say "Sure." Then they'd say, "Well, you can't!" I'd ask them why and they'd tell me, "You're not allowed to, that's why." So that's when I really found out about the law and the adoption records being sealed.

I think kids who are adopted should be allowed to know who their original parents are. It's a ridiculous law—that you're not allowed to know who they are unless a judge says it's OK. The records should be open for adoptees, and I don't think there should be an age restriction either. But if I ever did search, I'd do it on my own without telling my parents. I'd worry about hurting their feelings.

I've always had a picture in my mind of what my birthmother looks like. She's a little chubby, about thirty-seven years old, and

she's wearing a mink coat. I think I saw her once on Seventy-ninth and Broadway three years ago. I dream about her from time to time. She never changes—never gets older or anything like that.

I don't have one ounce of knowledge about my natural parents. Neither does my brother Philip—he's adopted too. It would be nice to know more, but I'm not all that frustrated about it. To tell you the truth, I don't think I'd go out of my way to find out who they are. I'd say the main thing I inherited from them is good teeth; I can't think of anything else.

I rarely talk about being adopted with my parents. I don't like to have personal discussions like that with them. In my health class we were talking about sex, and most of the kids said they felt awkward talking about such a personal matter with their parents. It's like that with me. Being adopted is a very private sort of thing. I don't mind discussing it with someone like a psychiatrist because that's different—a psychiatrist is there to help you and to discuss your feelings. It's funny, because my mother really is one, but I can't think of her that way. As far as I'm concerned, she's just my mother.

I'm very envious of kids who aren't adopted, who have natural parents—especially when they look like them. And I'm jealous because there are times when I think my original parents might be nicer than the ones I have now. I'm not saying my parents aren't nice because they are, but maybe my other parents wouldn't be so strict. Like maybe they wouldn't always be after me to clean up my room and do my homework. Sometimes, when I was growing up and my parents scolded me, I'd think about how they weren't my real parents, but I never said anything to them. Never will either.

Actually, lots of my friends are jealous of me. They think their parents are a pain and mine aren't, because I'm adopted and they had to go to so much trouble to get me. When I was little they'd all say, "Let's go over to Jack's house to play. He's adopted and his parents have to be nice to him."

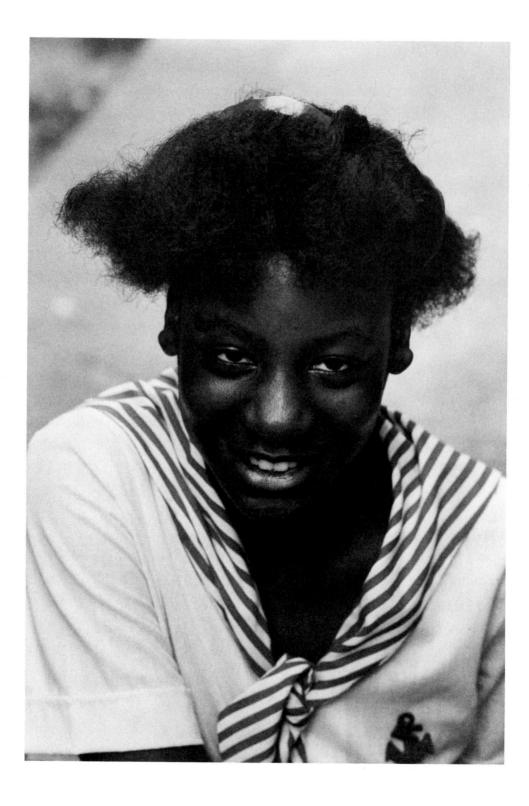

Gayle, age fourteen

My brother David and I are only four months apart in age—our parents brought us home on the same day. They had asked for twins, but the adoption agency didn't have any. When they got us, they already had adopted another son, Michael, who's four years older and both deaf and mute. I think it was good they adopted him because nobody else would do it. We don't even think of him as handicapped—to us, he's just a regular person who doesn't talk. And he hears what he wants to hear. I don't know how, but he does. I doubt if he knows that he's adopted.

When I was about four, my parents adopted another tiny baby named Teddy. He's paralyzed, but he can understand everything and he talks well enough that we can understand him. For example, when he holds up one finger it means he wants to eat and two fingers means he wants his Mommy. Now that he's eleven, he goes to a special school where they're teaching him how to talk better—I mean really talk the way normal people do. He's about the most lovable little boy I've ever seen and I thank God for sending him our way.

73

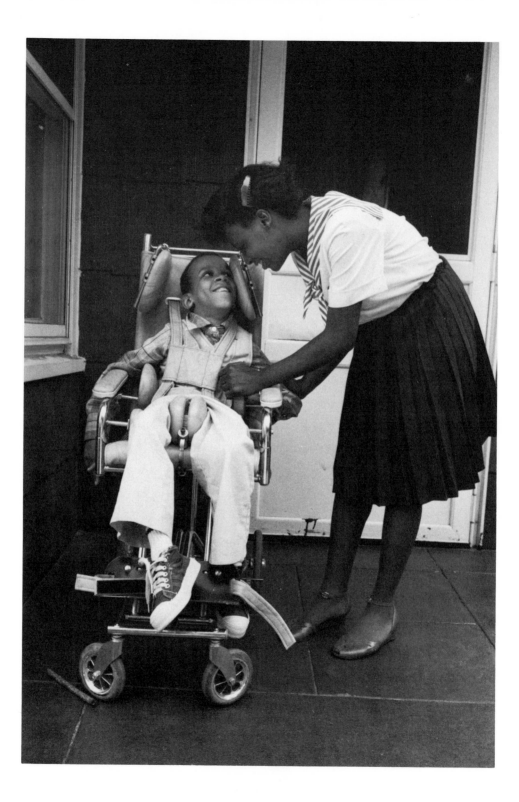

When I was six, my father died from cancer. I was too young to understand what was going on—all I knew was that there was an empty bed in the house. Now that I'm older, I'm especially glad that Mom adopted all of us, not just because she's given us a wonderful home, but because I know we've kept her from being too lonely. There aren't too many lonely times around our house, you can be sure of that! There's never a dull moment!

I didn't find out I was adopted until I was ten. Some of my friends started asking me how in the world I could have a brother who was born in June if I was born in September. I was curious too—about how this could be—and that's when my Mom explained that my real mother had put me up for adoption because she had too many problems. I don't think it made any difference to me not knowing the truth before then because I probably would have been too young to really understand. I didn't care when I found out and I don't care now. I'm happy the way things are.

I don't know much about my real parents except that my birthmother was about thirty and working as a secretary when I was born. I've been told she was real smart, well educated, and cute. I'd like to know more, particularly information about her nationality—like if she's of West Indian or African descent. I'd like to meet her someday, whenever she's ready to come by. This is the first year I've given it much thought, and I wonder if she'd like to meet me too. Mom says that every mother who gives birth to a baby loves it, but that somewhere down the line my real mother couldn't take care of me. Mom understands my curiosity and tells me if I ever do meet her that's fine with her—no hurt feelings on her part. She says all she ever wanted to do was

bring us up as law-abiding citizens and nice people. And she wanted to give us a good education and plenty of love. After that, as far as she's concerned, we're on our own.

My Mom is truly amazing. She's seventy-one and you'd never know it. In the morning she's up before any of us—usually around five o'clock—and I don't know when she goes to bed. In between taking care of all of us she works as a home attendant, looking after old people. Mama says that the Lord has answered all her prayers by sending her so many wonderful children—that her heart rejoices each and every day. As she puts it: "All these kids—they either make you young or they kill you." But she loves her life, and we sure love her!

Jane, age sixteen

I know I was about five years old when my parents first told me about my being adopted. It was just before I went to kindergarten. Then, when I was eight or nine, I used to read a book we had, called *The Chosen Baby*, and it made me wonder about who my real parents were and where they lived. By the time I was twelve, I had thought about it a lot and figured I'd probably do some searching when I got older.

I have an older brother who's also adopted, but he never wants to talk with me about that part of his life. I think boys who are adopted don't let themselves think about it because they feel the need to be tough. So I was feeling very alone, and when I went to bed at night, it took me a while to get to sleep. I'd just lie there and wonder what my real mother was like. Or I'd imagine that I'd already met her and not known it. Things like that.

One reason I was always thinking about my background is that when I was five, I developed epilepsy and the specialists were always asking questions about my medical history. My father and my doctor both wrote to the adoption agency requesting additional medical data, but the agency people never responded. We had very little information and it was extremely frustrating.

I was fifteen and it was in early December when my birthmother, Lorraine, phoned and spoke to my mother. The first time she called, Lorraine pretended she was conducting a survey for *Seventeen* magazine. It was around dinner time, and I was in the family room doing my homework. Mom was in the kitchen and I answered the phone, but the questions were a little confusing so I put my mother on the phone. Mom told the caller that I had a learning disability and she answered a couple of questions, but since she was in the middle of preparing dinner she didn't talk for very long.

That very same night, at approximately nine-thirty, the phone rang again. A woman asked to speak to my mother and I went upstairs to get ready for bed. It turned out to be the same lady who had said she was from *Seventeen*, except that this time she told my Mom: "On April 5, 1966, I gave birth to a daughter in Rochester, New York, whom I put up for adoption. I have reason to believe Jane is that child."

Mom told Lorraine that she was glad to hear from her and they talked for about half an hour. I wasn't aware of what was going on until Daddy came into my room and told me who was on the phone. He asked me if I would like to talk to her and even though I was stunned I said yes. Lorraine and I talked for about twenty minutes and the conversation was very weird. She told me a lot about her family, but it was hard for me to concentrate and I can't remember what we really talked about. After we hung up, my parents and I talked for a while, and then about an hour later we called Lorraine back and invited her and her husband to visit with us. Lorraine mentioned she would be coming to the Midwest during the Christmas holidays, but that didn't seem like a good idea to us so we suggested she wait until January. However, the next morning Lorraine called and said she would like to fly in on Saturday morning—which was only two days away! Even though my parents felt it was a little too soon for a visit—that we needed some time to adjust to this idea—my Mom said all right because I was eager to meet my birthmother and of course she could hardly wait to meet me. She had worked so hard to find me, we could easily imagine how excited she was.

For the next couple of days, we all spent a lot of time talking and reassuring each other. My mother was especially nervous because she felt extremely threatened. She told a few close friends what was happening, and most of them were against it, saying that she was too trusting and too foolish. My friends also disapproved and said things like "I wouldn't let her just walk into your life. You should tell her to buzz off!" But we're a really close family and all of us decided we loved each other and nothing could interfere with that love.

On Saturday morning, Dad and I went to the airport to meet Lorraine's plane. I saw a woman standing there looking around, not knowing where to go, so we figured it was her. I expected her to be taller because I'm tall for my age. She gave me a big hug, but I didn't know how to react so I kept my hands in my pockets. I felt a little awkward. In the car she asked me a lot of questions like what were my favorite subjects and what did I like to do. It seemed like having another grandmother visit because she was asking all those routine grandmother questions.

We spent the whole weekend at our house, mostly talking, and we showed each other photographs. Lorraine had brought a lot of family pictures with her, and I showed her several albums of my childhood. We stayed at home all day Saturday, and on Sunday we went to church and walked around the shopping center. One of the things we talked about—and giggled over—is that we had both spent hours deciding what we should wear for our big meeting. As it turned out, I wore jeans and she wore slacks.

Lorraine left on Monday morning after a nice visit and I went back to school. Later that month, the day after Christmas, I flew out to Detroit by myself to meet Lorraine's family and I stayed two days. Lorraine actually lives in New York, but her mother lives in Detroit, which is why we got together there. It was the first time I'd ever been on a plane, so I was probably as thrilled about that as anything else. They had a big family gathering which included Lorraine's husband, her mother, her two brothers, and lots of other relatives, but I was too overwhelmed by it and felt uncomfortable. Everyone treated me like a relative, which bothered me because I didn't feel that way. At one point, someone who was talking to me referred to Lorraine as "your Mom" and I didn't like that at all and said so. If I hadn't said anything I would have felt guilty and that wouldn't have helped anyone in the long run.

For the next few months, we wrote letters back and forth and Lorraine called me a few times, and then this Easter I flew up to New York for twelve days—the longest visit we'd ever had. This was the first time we really got to know each other and both of us had a wonderful time. She took me to Rockefeller Center to see the Easter lilies and we went to the ballet. We also visited lots of museums and tall buildings, but what I liked best was our just getting to know each other. One of the best things about my visit with Lorraine is that now I understand the problems she had before I was born and why she put me up for adoption. In a way, being adopted had always made me feel a little insecure, and even though I loved my parents, I still had a lot of unanswered questions and strange fantasies. Actually, one of my fantasies turned out to be true. I'd always imagined my birthmother was a writer, and that's exactly what Lorraine is. She writes for a lot of magazines and a few years ago she even wrote a book called *Birthmark* about what it was like to give me up. I still can't get over that!

The most upsetting part of our conversations was learning that she had written to the adoption agency in Rochester several times asking if my parents wanted any more medical information. They always told her no, even though my doctors had been asking—and begging—for updates because of my epilepsy. Luckily, however, that's all been taken care of. The important thing is that we've met and that now we can get to know each other better and better.

My Mom says I'm much more self-assured these days and that *she* also feels more secure. We all feel that my meeting Lorraine has added a new dimension to our relationship. It's as if we're a family now because we *want* to be—not just because we don't have a choice.

I haven't met my birthfather and I don't know if I will. Lorraine has told me a few things about him—such as he's a good chess player and he's Irish. My adoptive mother is also Irish, so every year she's made a big deal out of St. Patrick's Day. As I was growing up, I always asked her if I was Irish and she would tell me that she really didn't know because the agency had told her very little about my background. Well, now we know for sure that I'm Irish too, so this year I wore green like everyone else!

Pattie, age fifteen

I was adopted when I was five days old. My birthmother was about sixteen or seventeen, and as soon as she found out she was going to have me, she planned to give me up for adoption. Every time I hear about a girl my age who gets pregnant, I can't help thinking: This is the same thing that happened to my mother. I think my birthmother made the right decision, but it still makes me angry—not that she gave me up, but that she took the initial risk. It's too high a price to pay for being careless. I also feel very sorry for her because I imagine she didn't have any choice about keeping me at the time, and now that she's older, she probably feels guilty about giving me up.

I have a brother and a sister who are both adopted, and that makes it a lot easier. If they weren't both adopted like me, I know I'd feel a little out of place, as if I didn't really belong here. Even now, when I get really mad at my parents, I'm apt to think I don't belong where I am—like, I should be with my real mother.

It's also hard for me whenever somebody tells me I look just like my Mom. That kind of remark often makes me wish that I really was with my birthmother.

My biggest problem with being adopted is that I feel guilty I'm not more athletic, for the sake of my father. He's a wonderful athlete—he plays tennis and volleyball, and he used to coach softball—and I can't help wondering if he's thinking: Well, if I had some kids of my own. Like, maybe they would have inherited his natural ability. I've always tried to be good at sports, but somehow I always end up being a cheerleader.

I think adoptees should have the right to search if they want to. I read in "Dear Abby" that there's an agency called Origins which will help you, but you have to be eighteen. My mother and I talk about it a lot, and she says that if I want to look for my birthmother when I'm a little older, she'll help me. Agencies should give out more updated information to adoptees, and to their birthparents, too, if they want it. If I were a birthmother, I'd like to know that my child was happy.

If I do search one day, it'll be because in a way I feel as though a part of me is missing—a part that all my friends have. Even with my friends whose parents are divorced, and there's a situation where they don't see the father or the mother, at least they know who they are. With me, it's different. I don't have any idea who they are.

I've often thought about meeting my birthmother. If I found out where she was, I think I'd pretend that I was an Avon lady or something and go up to her house and just see how everything was. Then, after I had a chance to look things over and see what

she was like, that's when I could decide whether or not to tell her why I was really there. I always think about approaching her in that way. I know I wouldn't want to telephone her first or write her a letter.

If I do find her, it would be nice if we could just be friends, keeping in touch with one another from time to time. I wouldn't want any more of a relationship than that, because the mother I have now and I are so close. She's the one who's always taken care of me and listened to my problems, and she's the one who's always going to be there for me.

David, age eleven

I was in foster care for a while before my parents adopted me. I lived with a family that spoke Spanish, and they had two other foster kids. I don't remember that much about them. When my parents adopted me, they had to teach me English.

There's a note on the first page of my baby book that says:

> My Darling David,
>
> I wish that I could have gotten you sooner and not had to take you from another family where you were happy. But I'm glad to have you, and I feel sure that it won't take long for you to feel at home with us. I look forward to the day when you recognize me as, and call me, your mother.
>
> I am indeed delighted to at last have my David.
>
> Love,
> Mother

My birthmother was very young; that's why she put me up for adoption. I think she did what she thought would be best for me.

I don't talk about it very much with my parents because I worry that I'd hurt their feelings.

My sister's adopted, too, and everybody always talks about how beautiful she is, but it's kind of hard for me to think of her that way. I'm just like most of the kids I know—like, when I think their sisters are pretty, they just say they're ugly. Same thing with me.

I'm not all that curious about my birthfather. Sometimes, when I'm out playing baseball, or bowling, I wonder if he would be the kind of father my Dad is, out doing things with me. Stuff like that.

I hardly ever think about being adopted. Only at times, like on my birthday, and I imagine bumping into my real mother on the street. Once I dreamt that I was out on the sidewalk and it was my birthday and I was having a surprise party and she came up to me and just stopped and then we were talking and she said that eleven years ago she had given a child to an adoption agency. She looked very pretty. I'd like to meet her and see what she's like, and for her to see what I'm like, what I've grown up to be. I once asked my mother—I said I'd like to know who my real birthparents were, and she said, "Well, it's against the law to look." My mother said the laws existed because they think that the birthparents might want to take you back and they don't want that to happen. I don't think it would, because I like who I live with now. I love my parents and they love me! If I want to meet my birthparents, it's only because I'm curious and because I think it would be interesting. If you ask me, they should change the law.

Lulie, age sixteen

My twin brother and I were both adopted when we were about six months old. We were in foster homes because I was born with pneumonia and had to stay in the hospital for a while.

I've always known I was adopted. In fact, I don't remember not knowing. Being adopted was a subject which was always discussed openly and freely in our family. Of course, having a twin brother who was actually my own blood has made it a lot easier. I've always felt there's someone who is with me in every way— but maybe twins always feel like that.

I've been told that my birthparents were both really young and they were both working when we were born, which is why they put us up for adoption. I guess their jobs were very important to them and they just couldn't deal with twins at the time. My Mom thinks that they might have had something to do with the theater because my brother and I both have a lot of musical talent. I can sing, and my brother is really good at playing musical instruments. Sometimes I imagine my birthparents as being real famous, real stars!

Occasionally I walk along the street and think, Wow! Maybe one of these people is my parent! You know, especially when I visit a place like New York City. Other times I think I'm going to be somewhere and someone will say, "God, you look a lot like So-and-So," and she'll turn out to be my mother. I don't actually think about my birthfather as much.

I think adoption is a really good thing. If I got pregnant now, I would definitely put the baby up for adoption because I know it would be best for it. There's no way I could take care of a little baby. Last week I was baby-sitting for a little boy and it's just not the kind of situation I could deal with, day in and day out, especially if I wanted to keep on going to school. If I had a kid, I'd have to drop out and be a full-time mother, and I wouldn't want to do that.

I imagine it would be very easy for our birthmother to trace us, especially since we're twins, but I'm not sure I'd want her to. In a way, I'd really be curious to meet her, but I feel it would kind of hurt me to have her just come back into my life at this point and say, "Here I am!" I wouldn't want that at all. Even though I understand that she did what was best for us, there's still a part of me that feels rejected. In a way, though, I'd like to see what she looks like because I've had dreams about her and she always looks the same. If we ever do meet each other, I'd feel a lot less guilty if she found me than if I went looking for her. I suppose I'd be more apt to search if I wasn't worried about hurting the feelings of my parents. My Mom is more "Go ahead . . . do what you want . . . see who she is," but my Daddy would be really hurt.

I think that if an adopted child wants to search for a birthparent, he or she should have that right, even if the birthparent doesn't want to be found. They're the ones who gave me up in the first place, and I had nothing to do with it at the time. I also feel that if either one of them wants to look for me and I don't want to be found, it is my right to say no.

A lot of people say I shouldn't try to find my real parents, especially people who are parents themselves. But my friends who are my age say I should, and they've all offered to help me. I think it's really neat that they're all so involved with my life.

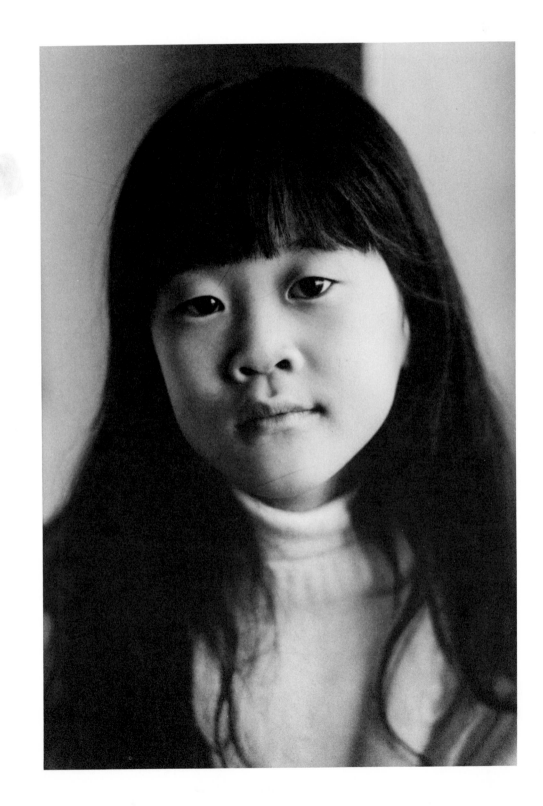

Soo-Mee, age eight

We have some pictures of the day I arrived in New York from Korea. I came with five other children, and a nun and two priests took care of us on the plane. I have a photograph of my Mom at the airport hugging me and looking very happy. I was three years old.

When I arrived here, I had a little package of some Korean clothes and shoes. I still have them, and the clothes I wore on the plane, and it's fun to look at them. It's hard to believe I was ever that little. I also had a folder with my passport and birth certificate and lots of other papers. I look at them whenever I want. There's a picture of me with the Korean foster mother I lived with for eight months. When I was littler I always asked my Mom, "Did they send me away because I was bad?" And she would show me a letter from the Korean agency that says, "Soo-Mee is a lovely child who brings lots of joy to all of us." That always made me feel much better.

The day after my fifth birthday, we went to court with a lawyer to make everything legal. That means nobody can take me away

from Mommy until I'm grown up and ready to go on my own. The judge had tears in her eyes and she said, "This is such a lovely story." I had to sign some papers, and when the judge asked me my name, I said, "My name is Soo-Mee." Afterwards, Mommy and I went to a friend's house for lunch, and the grownups had champagne. That evening, my godparents had a special dinner just for us, and they gave me a silver vase with one red rose in it.

When I lost my parents and came here from Korea, I didn't understand what was happening, and I didn't really think about it.

Now that I'm older, I sometimes feel that my whole life started when I was three years old.

I'd like to visit Korea when I get older. My Mommy showed me where it is on the globe. I have two Korean dolls, and once we went to a Korean restaurant, and I liked the food.

I wish I could remember my real-real-real parents and know what they look like, but the Mommy I have is terrific and I love her a lot. She's my real Mommy now, and we're good cuddle-bugs. There's only one little problem, which is that I'd like my Mommy to get married so I could have a Daddy too.

Joey, age fourteen

I lived with my mother until I was eleven, but it got to the point where she couldn't handle me and so she awarded me to the state—that's how I came to live at the orphanage. She kept my three sisters, but since she's no longer my mother, I don't think of them as my sisters anymore either. I never knew my father because he just walked out on us—I was only a baby at the time so I don't even remember what he looked like. I can't say I'm mad at him, because I don't know him and I don't know what his reasons were.

Luckily, I only had to stay in the orphanage for about a year. What happened is that about two years ago, around Thanksgiving, a Catholic priest named Father Clements was trying to get his parishioners, who were mostly black, to adopt black kids who needed homes. No one was paying any attention to him, so he finally said, "Well, if you won't adopt, then I will!" Two weeks before Christmas he got a call from the director of the orphanage saying there was a twelve-year-old boy named Joey he might like to meet. Father Clements thought it would be nice to invite me to his house for Christmas dinner, but when he asked me I said I had to think about it because I had a lot of other invitations from family and friends. I was lying because I had too much pride to let him think I didn't have any place to go. And it was my pride which actually impressed this priest and made him come back to see me again and again.

One day we went to the airport with his sister, who had to catch a plane somewhere, and while we were waiting she asked me to go and buy her a newspaper. Right there on the front page of the Chicago *Sun Times* was a picture of Father Clements and a story about his wanting to adopt a child. I was wondering if that kid might turn out to be me, but I didn't say anything—I just brought back the paper. On the way home Father Clements asked me if I had read it, and when I said "no," he pulled over to the side of the road. He put his arm around me and said that if we were going to have any kind of relationship at all, we had to begin by being honest with each other. So I admitted I'd read the story about him, and that's when he told me that he was going to adopt me. I started crying because I was so happy, and Father Clements thought I was crying because I didn't want him to adopt me, but we got everything straightened out and a few days later I moved in with him. It was two days before Christmas and I've been there ever since. That was the best Christmas I've ever had. The only part I didn't like was that all his relatives had gifts for me and I felt ashamed because I didn't have any for them.

There's been a lot of publicity about my being adopted by a priest, but it's hard for me to understand all the commotion—

after all, what's the difference between having a priest for a father or having a doctor or a lawyer? As long as there's love and caring, that's all that matters. What's important is to get kids out of institutions and into homes. As far as I'm concerned, all homeless kids should be adopted by anyone who really wants them, regardless of race, color or creed or whether they're married or not. I know that whenever I used to dream about being adopted, all I hoped for was a loving home. Period. I just wanted to be adopted so I could start a new life for myself, and that's exactly what I've been able to do. Now I have someone to love and someone who loves me. We take care of each other and have those special feelings that are part of being a family. The way I see it, that's all that matters.

There were several books about adoption that I found particularly helpful and I list them here so they might benefit others.

Is That Your Sister? by Sherry and Catherine Bunin: Pantheon, 1976. A picture book for young children about interracial adoption.

Quintana & Friends by John Gregory Dunne: Pocket Books, 1980. The author discusses his feelings as an adoptive parent in the first essay.

Birthmark by Lorraine Dusky: M. Evans, 1979. A birthmother's story.

I'm Still Me by Betty Jean Lifton: Knopf, 1981; Bantam, 1982. A young-adult novel about a teenager who searches.

Lost and Found by Betty Jean Lifton: Dial Press, 1979; Bantam, 1981. A comprehensive study about adoption by an adult adoptee.

Twice Born by Betty Jean Lifton: McGraw-Hill, 1975; Penguin Books, 1977. A memoir about growing up adopted.

They Came to Stay by Marjorie Margolis and Ruth Gruber: Coward, McCann & Geoghegan, 1976. A single parent adopts two little girls, one Korean and one Vietnamese.

Aaron's Door by Miska Miles: Little, Brown, 1978. An illustrated book for young children that describes the feelings of a young boy entering an adoptive home.

Successful Adoption by Jacqueline Hornor Plumez: Harmony Books, 1982. A comprehensive guide for finding a child and raising a family.

So You're Adopted by Fred Powledge: Charles Scribner's Sons, 1982. An honest book for adolescents about the experience of being adopted.

The Adoption Triangle by Arthur D. Sorosky, Annette Baran, and Reuben Pannor: Anchor Press, Doubleday, 1978; Anchor Books, 1979. A good psychological study for adults.

Special thanks to:

Jody Eastman, Rocco Staino, Dotsie Salituri, Deborah Dougherty, Stephani Cook, Valerie Crowley, Marilyn Herbert, Lorraine Dusky, Joanne Hiscox, Ricky Lauren, Sue Gustavson, and Alison Ward, who put me in touch with many of the young people in this book.

Claire Berman, Betty Jean Lifton, Dr. Arnold Cooper, James Green, Jane Edwards, Viola Bernard, Ruby Lee Piester, Bill Pierce, Marietta Spencer, Erna Furman, and Eda LeShan, who shared with me their diverse opinions about adoption.

Dr. Susan Baker, my good friend, for her perceptive insights, good advice, and constant encouragement.

Carol Atkinson, who, as usual, transcribed with speed and intelligence all the tapes of my interviews.

Everyone at Knopf, especially Martha Kaplan, Bob Gottlieb, Sara Reynolds, John Woodside, and Dennis Dwyer.

J.K.

A NOTE ON THE TYPE

This book was set on the Linotype in Granjon, a type named in compliment to Robert Granjon. It is neither a copy of a classic face nor an entirely original creation. George W. Jones based his designs for this type on that used by Claude Garamond (1510–61) in his beautiful French books, and Granjon more closely resembles Garamond's own type than do any of the various modern types that bear his name.

Composed by Maryland Linotype Composition Company, Inc., Baltimore, Maryland. Printed and bound by The Murray Printing Company, Westford, Massachusetts.

*The design of this book is an adaptation
by Sara Reynolds of a design
by Dorothy Schmiderer.*